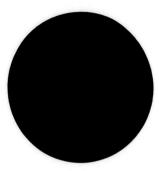

BELLY
LAUGH
HILARIOUS
School's out for Summer
JOKES
for Kids

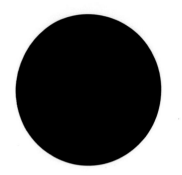

BELLY LAUGH HILARIOUS

School's out for Summer

JOKES

for Kids

350 Hilarious Summer Jokes!

Sky Pony Press
New York

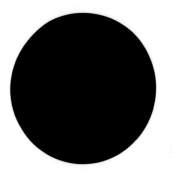

Sky Pony Press books may be purchased in bulk at special discounts for sales promotion, corporate gifts, fund-raising, or educational purposes. Special editions can also be created to specifications. For details, contact the Special Sales Department, Sky Pony Press, 307 West 36th Street, 11th Floor, New York, NY 10018 or info@skyhorsepublishing.com.

Sky Pony® is a registered trademark of Skyhorse Publishing, Inc.®, a Delaware corporation.

Visit our website at www.skyponypress.com.

10 9 8 7 6 5 4 3 2 1

Manufactured in China, 2019
This product conforms to CPSIA 2008

Library of Congress Cataloging-in-Publication Data is available on file.

ISBN: 978-1-5107-4322-9
EISBN: 978-1-5107-4326-7

Cover design by Daniel Brount
Illustrations by Alex Paterson

Printed in China

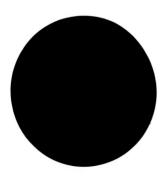

BELLY LAUGH HILARIOUS

School's out for Summer

JOKES

for Kids

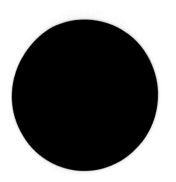

Knock, Knock!

Who's there?

Noah!

Noah who?

Noah more school until September!

☆

Knock, Knock!

Who's there?

Wendy!

Wendy who?

Wendy bell rings, school's out for summer!

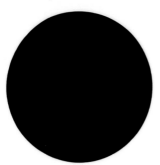

Knock, Knock!

Who's there?

Gladys!

Gladys who?

Gladys the last day of school!

Knock, knock!

Who's there?

Orange!

Orange who?

Orange you glad that it's summer?

What did the teacher say to the parents on the last day of school?

Tag! You're it!

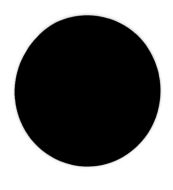

Why did the broom have to go to summer school?

Because it was always caught sweeping in class!

What students never miss class during the summer?

All of them, because nobody misses classes during the summer!

Who goes to boarding school during the summer?

Surfers!

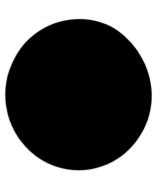

Why is a closed school in

summer liked closed eyes?

There aren't any pupils to see!

When do students get scolded for something

they didn't do?

When they don't do their homework!

What did the boy say when the teacher gave

him his June report card?

Do you want me to sign it now or later?

What wears a uniform and floats?

A buoy scout!

If you're in the forest and there's a fork in the trail, what do you do?

Pick it up and use it when you have lunch!

If a flea and a fly pass it other, what time is it?

Fly past flea!

It's so hot that I saw two

trees chasing a dog!

☆

It's so hot that trees are looking for shade!

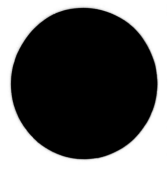

What is a twip?

A twip is what a wabbit takes when he wides a twain!

What did the student say when the teacher asked him to pay a little attention on the last day of school?

He told her he was paying as little attention as he could!

Why don't fish go on vacation?

They're always in schools!

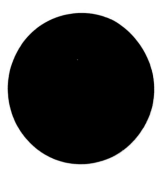

What's the best card game

to play on a boat?

Go Fish!

Why was the teacher cross-eyed at the end of

the school year?

He had lost control of his pupils!

What school do kids want to go to during the

summer?

Sundae school for the ice cream!

Why did the whale cross the ocean?

To get to the other tide!

☆

 What game can you play on a boat?

Cards - because there's always a deck around!

☆

Why was the fish alone at the bottom of the ocean?

Because he dropped out of his school!

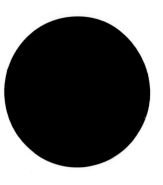

Why do fish live in salt water?

Because pepper makes them sneeze!

Why are mosquitoes annoying?

Because they get under your skin!

☆

Why did the teacher go to the beach?

He wanted to test the water!

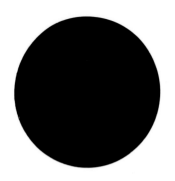

What kind of fish can't swim?

A dead one!

Did you hear the joke about the mountain?

It's hard to get over it!

What are the rules in zebra baseball?

Three stripes and you're out!

Where do swimmers clean themselves?

They wash up on shore!

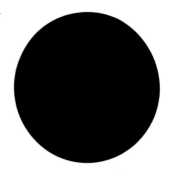

How do pandas stay cool in

the summer?

They use bear-conditioning!

Where do shrimp borrow money?

From the prawn broker!

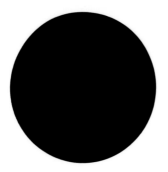

What did the boy say after a

long day at the beach?

"I'm surf bored!"

What do sharks eat for dinner?

Fish and ships!

What do you call a witch that lives at the

beach?

A sand witch!

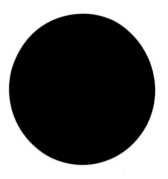

Where does Bugs Bunny

keep his boat?

At the What's Up Dock?

What did the man say when he crashed his boat

into a dock?

It a-piers we have a problem!

Why was the baseball player a bad sport?

He stole third base and then went home!

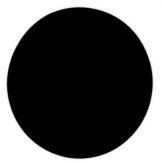

Why don't oysters share their pearls?

They're shellfish!

Why did Mickey Mouse go into space for his vacation?

He was looking for Pluto!

What do Christmas and a cat at the beach have in common?

Sandy claws!

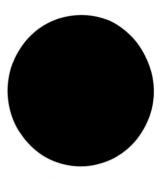

Why did the motorboat

become friendly with the

sailboat?

Because he liked her a yacht!

Why didn't the dog play baseball?

Because it was a boxer!

What word looks the same backwards and

upside down?

SWIMS!

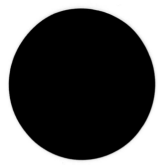

Did you hear the joke about the watermelon?

It's pit-iful!

Where do ants go out to dinner?

To restaur-ants!

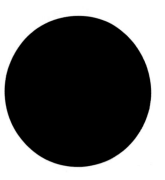

Why did the policeman go to the beach?

Something fishy was going on!

What's the baseball's favorite part of the playground?

The swings!

Why can't children go to pirate movies?

Because they are rated Arrrrrrrr!

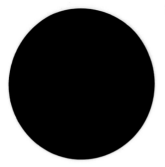

I haven't been to the beach in years—long time, no sea!

How does a witch select a hotel?

The one with the best broom service!

What happens when you take a clock on an airplane?

Time flies!

What sailing movie starred

Darth Vader?

Starboard!

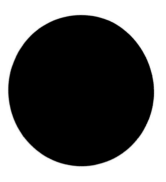

How do you get wrinkles out of a sail?

With boat-tox!

What vegetable is green and goes to summer

camp?

A Brussels scout!

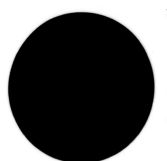

How do you communicate with a fish?

Drop it a line!

☆

Why was the baseball player arrested?

He stole second base!

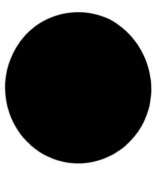

Where do fish borrow money?

From loan sharks!

Why shouldn't fish eat worms?

Because they'll get hooked on them!

What did the fish say when he won the lottery?

It was just a fluke!

☆

What do you call an ant that skips school?

A tru-ant!

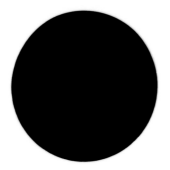

What do you call a strong shellfish?

A mussel!

What kind of jacket is good for hiking?

A trail blazer!

What sandwiches can you make at the beach?

Peanut butter and jellyfish!

How do you prevent a summer cold?

Stop it in the winter!

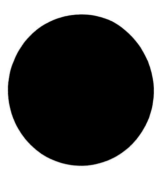

What's an orca's favorite TV show?

Whale of Fortune!

What did the shark say after eating a clown fish?

That tasted funny!

Why did the chicken cross the playground?

To get to the other slide!

☆

What did the confused shark say?

Could you be more Pacific?

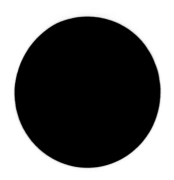

What dries as it gets wetter?

A towel!

What do you call a group of Jennifers in a pool?

Hydro-jens!

How did the shark plead in court?

Not gill-ty!

☆

How does a boat get over a cold?

With vitamin sea!

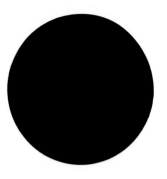

Why are pigs bad at soccer?

They hog the ball!

Why do you bring baseball gear to a boat?

To batten down the hatches!

Why is the letter "A" like a flower?

Because bees come after them!

What's a good dessert for the summertime?

Beach pie!

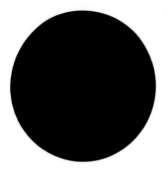

Did you hear about the ant that won the Nobel prize?

The call him brilli-ant!

Why did the soccer ball quit the team?

It was tired of being kicked around!

Why are people who go camping on April Fool's Day so tired?

They just finished a 31-day March!

What kind of baseball do

they play in England?

Tea-ball!

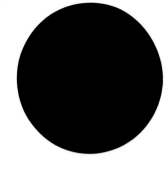

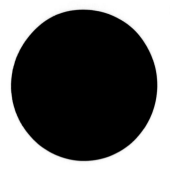

Knock, Knock!

Who's there?

Cargo!

Cargo who?

Car go beep beep!

What's worse than finding a worm in your apple?

Finding half a worm!

How many trees can you plant in an empty field?

One. After that it's not empty anymore!

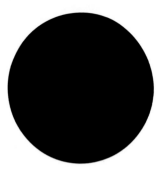

Why was the swimmer slow?

He was doing the crawl!

Where do fish keep their money?

In the river bank!

Why were the campers so exhausted?

The camp was in-tents!

When is a ship at sea not on water?

When it's on fire!

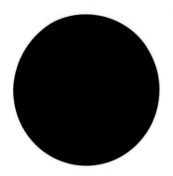

What do you tell a sick orca?

Get whale soon!

What did the pig say on a hot summer day?

I'm bacon!

What subject do runners like in school?

Jog-graphy!

Why are frogs good outfielders?

They catch flies!

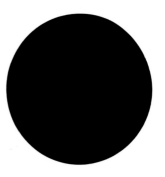

What sport do spiders like?

Fly fishing!

What is the biggest ant in the world?

An eleph-ant!

What do you call a snail in the Navy?

A snailor!

Why didn't the octopus's computer work?

There were tentacle difficulties!

What's smarter than a talking parrot?

A spelling bee!

What do you call two octopuses that look alike?

I-tentacle twins!

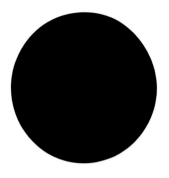

What do two ropes do when

they love each other?

They get hitched!

Why couldn't the butterfly go to the dance?

Because it was a moth ball!

Why are gulls called seagulls?

Because if they lived by the bay they'd be called

bagels!

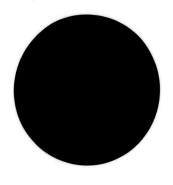

What do bees do when they get hot?

They take off their yellow jackets!

Have you heard the joke about the pop fly?

It's over your head!

What do you do if they charge admission to the beach?

Use sand dollars!

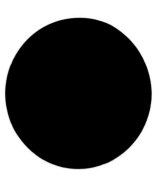

What did the fish say to her overzealous boyfriend?

We have to scale things back!

What did the boy octopus say to the girl octopus?

Can I hold your hand, hand, hand, hand, hand, hand, hand, hand?

What part of a stadium is never the same?

The changing rooms!

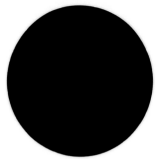

Why was Cinderella a bad soccer player?

Her coach was a pumpkin!

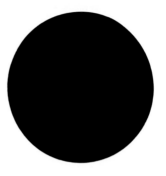

What's the saltiest letter?

The "C!"

What do you call a baby whale?

A little squirt!

What do you call a fly without wings?

A walk!

☆

What did one volcano say to the other volcano?

I lava you!

What do frogs wear on their feet in the summer?

Open toad shoes!

What kind of hair does the ocean have?

Wavy!

What's brown and hairy with sunglasses?

A coconut on vacation!

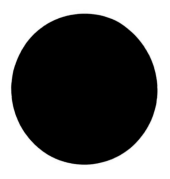

What do fish wear in

aquariums?

Tank tops!

What do you call ice cream on a very hot day?

Cream!

☆

What kind of fish has two knees?

A tu-knee fish!

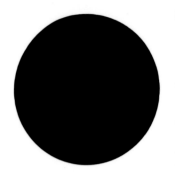

Why did the summer school teacher wear sunglasses?

Her students were very bright!

What is a mosquito's favorite sport?

Skin diving!

What do sheep do in the summertime?

Have baa-baa cues!

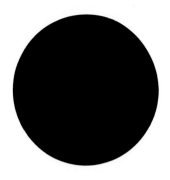

What direction do chickens swim?

Cluck-wise!

How can you tell that elephants like vacations?

They always have their trunks ready!

How do you catch a squirrel?

Climb up a tree and act like a nut!

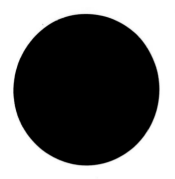

What do sea monsters like to eat?

Ships and dips!

Where can seaweed look for a job?

In the kelp wanted section!

How do you catch a monkey?

Climb a tree and act like a banana!

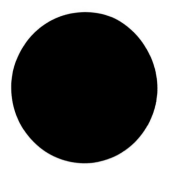

What do they have at tiny beaches?

Micro-waves!

Why do soccer players do well in school?

They use their heads!

What do you say when the beach asks you to walk on it?

Shore!

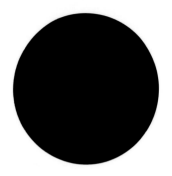

What's a drowned report card?

Under C level!

What do you call a wasp?

A wanna-bee!

☆

What do you call a girl at the beach?

Sandy!

☆

How do you cut the ocean in half?

With a sea-saw!

Why shouldn't you tell a

whale a secret?

Because they're blubber mouths!

How did the campers like the campfire?

They gave it glowing reviews!

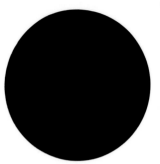

Knock, Knock!

Who's there?

Dawn!

Dawn who?

Dawn wake me up so early!

What did the carp say to his girlfriend?

Don't play koi with me!

What's the difference between an unhappy

baseball player and a marine biologist?

One wails and catches, the other catches whales!

How does the sun drink water?

With sun glasses!

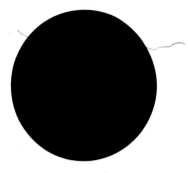

What do you call a poodle at the beach in July?

A hot dog!

Why did the boat crash into the dock?

It was closer than it a-piered!

How did the flea go on vacation?

Itch-hiking!

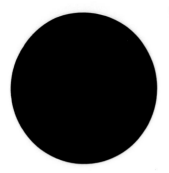

Who cleans the ocean?

The mer-maids!

What do you get when you cross a baseball player and a tree?

Babe Root!

What happens when two fish disagree?

They don't sea things the same way!

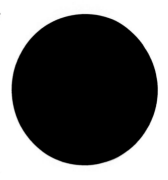

What do frogs drink in the summer?

Croak-a-cola!

What exercise do swimmers do?

Pool-ups!

How do you make a man with one arm fall out of a tree?

Wave!

How are people on a hot day like a piece of clothing?

They're sweaters!

What do you call a bug jumping over drinking cups?

A glass-hopper!

What's a famous fish called?

A star-fish!

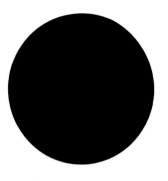

What do sardines call submarines?

Cans of people!

How does an octopus fight?

Fully armed!

☆

Why did the vegetarian quit the swimming team?

She didn't like meets!

Why don't basketball players take vacations?

They'll get called for traveling!

What fish grants wishes?

The fairy cod-mother!

What does a baseball player use to bake a cake?

Batter, Bunt pans, and oven Mitts!

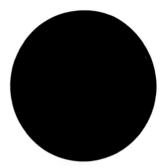

Where do cows go for

entertainment?

The moo-vies!

Did you hear about the restaurant for dolphins?

It serves a porpoise!

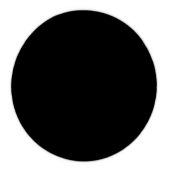

What do you get when you cross a cow and an octopus?

An animal that can milk itself!

How do trees go on the internet?

They log in!

Where do sheep go on vacation?

The Baa-hamas!

Where do ants go on vacation?

Ant-lantic City!

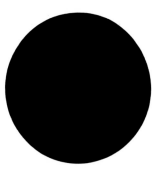

What do you get when you throw a yellow tennis ball in the Red Sea?

A wet tennis ball!

☆

Where do pepperonis go on vacation?

The leaning tower of Pizza!

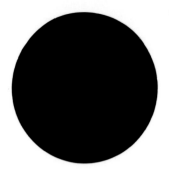

What swimming stroke goes well on toast?

The butter-fly!

Where do cows go on vacation?

Moo York City!

Where do ghosts go on vacation?

Lake Eerie!

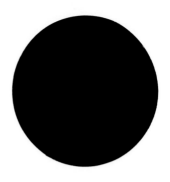

Where do orcas go on vacation?

Wales!

How does a warm ocean say hello?

With a heat wave!

Where does a cow stay on vacation?

A moo-tel!

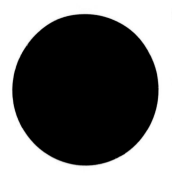

Where do eggs go on vacation?

New Yolk City!

Where do crayons go on vacation?

Color-ado!

Where do math teachers go on vacation?

Math-achussetts!

Where do werewolves stay on vacation?

At the Howl-iday Inn!

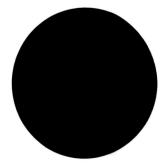

Where do pencils go on

vacation?

Pencil-vania!

☆

Where do lawyers go on vacation?

Sue York City!

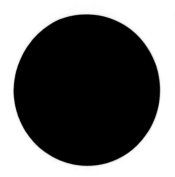

Where do ants go on vacation?

Fr-ants!

Where did the ant go after Fr-ants?

Antwerp!

Where do teachers go on vacation?

Times Square!

Where do pianists go on vacation?

The Florida Keys!

Where do bees go on vacation?

Sting-apore!

Where do birds go on vacation?

The Canary Islands!

Where do fish go on vacation?

Fin-land!

Where do goldfish go on vacation?

Around the globe!

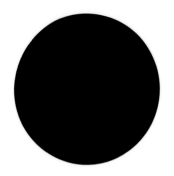

Where do hamsters go on vacation?

Hamster-dam!

Where do zombies go on vacation?

The Dead Sea!

What kind of dives do they do in the army?

Cannonballs!

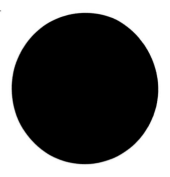

Where do fleas go on

vacation?

Search me!

How do you start a firefly race?

Ready, set, glow!

Why did the hotel receptionist give the guest a

candy?

Because he asked for a suite!

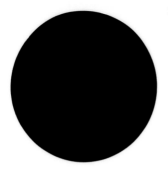

Why did the baseball player shut down his web site?

He wasn't getting any hits!

Two waves had a race. Who won?

They tide!

What game do sheep play?

Baa-dminton!

What comes out of a

sprinkler on a hot day?

Steam!

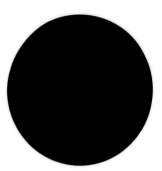

Where do seahorses live?

In BARN-acles!

Why did the vampires cancel the baseball game?

Because they couldn't find their bats!

Why did the chicken cross the basketball court?

Because the referee cried, "Fowl!"

What bites math teachers during the summer?

Mathema-ticks!

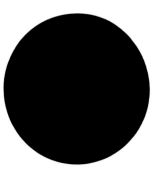

What are spider webs good for?

Spiders!

What's the difference between a piano and a fish?

You can tune a piano but you can't tuna fish!

How hot is it?

It's so hot you can't make a chili dog!

☆

Why shouldn't you swim on a full stomach?

Because it's easier to swim on water!

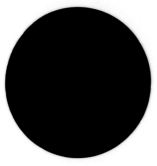

What do goblins send their friends when they are on vacation?

Ghost-cards!

What do one girl firefly say to the other girl firefly?

You glow girl!

What makes a firefly glow?

A light meal!

What superhero do you want

on your baseball team?

Batman!

Why was the firefly unhappy?

Because his children weren't that bright!

☆

What do you call an awesome octopus?

A tenta-cool guy!

☆

How do you know mosquitos are religious?

They prey on you!

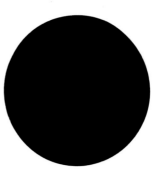

Why is it difficult for matches to play baseball?

One strike and you're out!

Why was my friend so tired after her vacation?

She flew home!

☆

What steps should you take if you see a dangerous animal in the woods?

Very large ones!

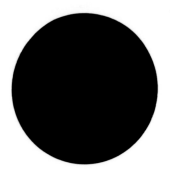

What do you call a snowman in August?

A puddle!

What did one bee say to the other on a hot day in the summer?

Swarm here!

When do baseball players wear armor?

For knight games!

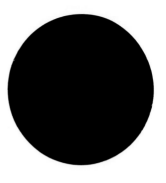

Where can you find an ocean

   without water?

On a map!

What did one firefly say to another?

Got to glow now!

What do you call a messy crayfish?

A slob-ster!

What's a knight's favorite fish?

A sword fish!

☆

Why did the fish cross the beach?

To get to the other tide!

Where do oysters sleep?

On a sea-bed!

Why couldn't the girl swim?

Lack of BOY-ancy!

What's the best season for addition?

Sum-mer!

What do you call a party at the beach?

A shell-ebration!

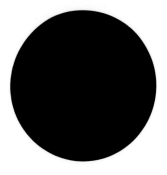

What do cows wear in Hawaii?

Moo-moos!

Why did the beach blush?

Because the sea weed!

What do you get when you cross a monster with a baseball player?

A double header!

Welcome to our _OOL!

Notice there's no "P" in it?

We like to keep it that way!

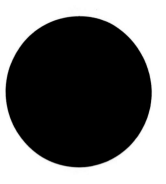

Have you ever seen a live drive?

No, but I've seen a baseball park!

What has eighteen legs and catches flies?

A baseball team!

Why wasn't the woman scared when she saw a shark swimming next to her?

It was a MAN-eating shark!

How do rabbits travel on their vacations?

Hare-planes!

What's the difference between a mosquito and a fly?

Try zipping a mosquito!

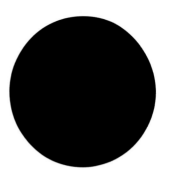

Knock, Knock!

Who's there?

Tennis!

Tennis who?

Ten is five plus five!

What kind of fish comes out at night?

A star-fish!

What does Cinderella wear to go swimming?

Glass flippers!

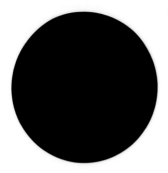

How do you find where a mosquito has bitten you?

Start from scratch!

What do you call a girl in the middle of a tennis court?

Annette!

Why does a baseball player raise one leg when he pitches?

If he raised both legs, he'd fall down!

How do clams call each other?

On shell phones!

☆

How do you weigh fish?

With scales!

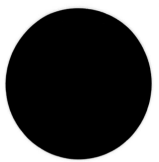

What did the bee say to the flower?

Hello, honey!

What do you call a boomerang that doesn't come back?

A stick!

How hot is it?

So hot that all of the bread in the supermarket is toast!

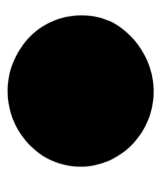

Why was it so hot in the ballpark after the game?

Because all of the fans left!

What do bees chew?

Bumble-gum!

Why does it take longer to run from second base to third base than from first base to second base?

Because there is a short stop in the middle!

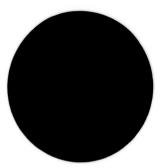

What comedian is popular on a hot day?

The Good Humor man!

Where do coal diggers play baseball?

In the miner leagues!

What do you call French sandals?

Philippe Phloppes!

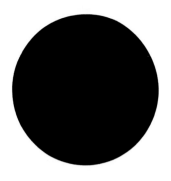

What is served but never

eaten?

A tennis ball!

Did you hear the joke about the tree?

It will leaf you laughing!

What did the baseball glove say to the baseball?

Catch you later!

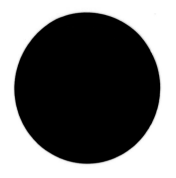

What's at the bottom of the ocean and twitches?

A nervous wreck!

What's stranger than seeing a cat fish?

Seeing a fish bowl!

Did you hear about the camper who broke his left arm and his left leg?

He's all right now!

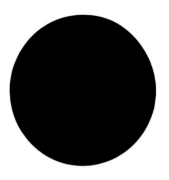

What do a dentist and a swimming coach have in common?

They both use drills!

Why did they play the baseball game at night?

Because the bats were sleeping during the day!

What's another name for a sleeping bag?

A nap-sack!

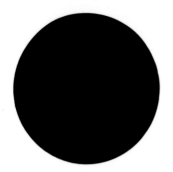

What do bears call campers

in sleeping bags?

Soft tacos!

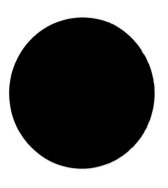

**If you have five sleeping
bags in one hand and
three backpacks in the
other, what do you have?**

Big hands!

Why do bees hum?

Because they don't know the words!

What did the ocean say to the boat?

Nothing. It just waved!

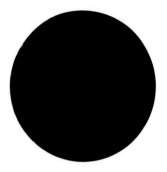

Why did the pine tree get into trouble?

Because it was knotty!

Where do saplings go to learn?

Elemen-tree school!

Why did the golfer where two pairs of pants?

In case he got a hole in one!

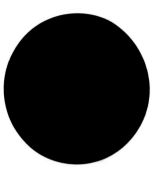

How hot is it?

So hot that the farmer is feeding

the chickens ice so they

won't lay hard-boiled eggs!

☆

How does the ocean say goodbye?

It waves!

☆

What animal is best at baseball?

A bat!

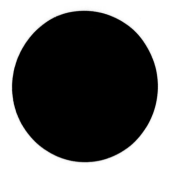

What do you do when you get cold while camping?

Go to the corner of the tent—it's normally 90 degrees!

What do baseball players eat on?

Home plates!

What lights up a soccer stadium?

A soccer match!

What did Obi Wan Kenobi

say to the tree?

May the forest be with you!

A man tried to sue a shark for biting off his

limbs, but he didn't have a leg to stand on!

What travels across the country but stays in one

corner?

A stamp!

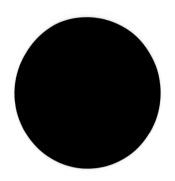

What's a fish without an eye?

A fsh!

What is the best day to go to the beach?

Sun-day!

Why do bananas use sunscreen?

Because they peel easily!

☆

What do you get if you cross ants and ticks?

All sorts of antics!

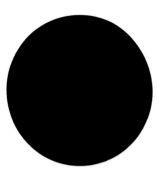

Which fish is worth the most?

A gold-fish!

Why didn't the skeleton play baseball?

His heart wasn't in it!

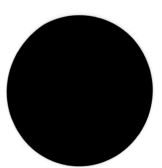

What's the coolest letter?

Iced-T!

How do you win a baseball game without any balls?

Throw only strikes!

What does bread do on vacation?

It just loafs around!

What do trees wear at the beach?

Their swimming trunks!

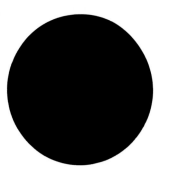

What's gray and has four legs and a trunk?

A mouse on vacation!

Why did the man swim the back stroke?

Because he just ate and didn't want to swim on a full stomach!

What relative comes to a picnic without being invited?

Ants!

What game do sharks like?

Swallow the leader!

☆

Why don't mummies take vacations?

They are afraid to relax and unwind!

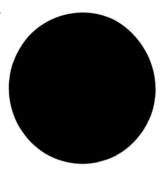

Knock, Knock!

Who's there?

Amos!

Amos who?

Amos-quito just bit me!

Why is a baseball team like pancakes?

They both need batters!

What detergent do you use for bathing suits?

Tide!

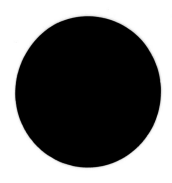

What fish live in heaven?

Angel fish!

Where shouldn't a baseball player wear red?

In the bull pen!

How hot is it?

So hot that the corn in the field is popping!

What do you call two crazy bugs on the moon?

Lunar-ticks!

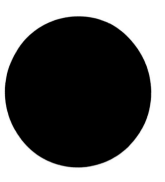

Where do you find a baseball catcher at dinner time?

Behind the plate!

What did the llama say when invited to the picnic?

Alpaca lunch!

Two fathers and two sons go fishing. They each catch a fish but only return with three fish. How?

They were a grandfather, a son, and a grandson!

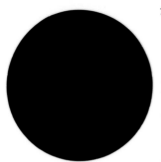

Knock, Knock!

Who's there?

Amy!

Amy who?

Amy-fraid of spiders!

Why was the river rich?

It had two banks!

Why did one baseball player call the other?

To touch base!

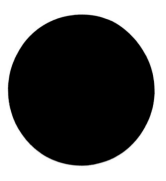

What did the clownfish say to her baby?

Keep your friends close and your anemones closer!

Where does a baseball player go buy a uniform?

New Jersey!

What did one tidal pool say to the other tidal pool?

Show me your mussels!

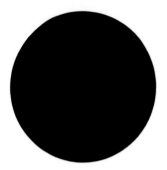

What's the hardest thing about parachuting?

The ground!

Which baseball player wears the biggest helmet?

The one with the biggest head!

What is a bear with no teeth called?

A gummy bear!

What side of a tree has the most leaves?

The outside!

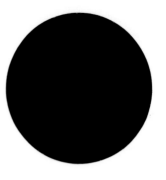

Did you hear about the duck

on the baseball team?

It only throws fowl balls!

What did the seaweed say when it was in trouble?

Kelp! Kelp!

What's a ghost's favorite soccer position?

Ghoul-keeper!

Why wasn't Cinderella good at soccer?

She ran away from the ball!

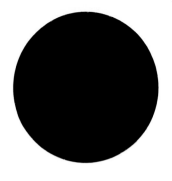

What happened when the red ship crashed into the blue ship?

Everyone was marooned!

Why are umpires fat?

Because they always clean their plate!

What did the newspaper reporter say to the ice cream?

Have I got a scoop for you!

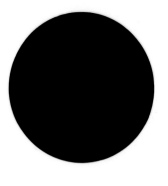

Knock, Knock!

Who's there?

Arthur!

Arthur who?

Arthur any bears at this camp?

☆

What do you call an elephant in a bathing suit?

Swimming trunks!

☆

Did you hear about the kidnapping at the beach?

It's okay. He woke up!

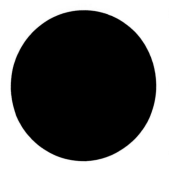

What do you call a camper with a nose and no body?

Nobody knows!

What's fuzzy and green and would kill you if it fell on you?

A pool table!

When do you go at red and stop at green?

When eating watermelon!

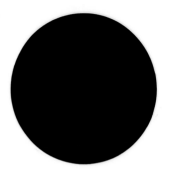

Why didn't the bike go on vacation?

It was two-tired!

☆

How do bees go on vacation?

They take the buzz!

☆

How do you know baseball players are rich?

They play on diamonds!

Knock, Knock!

Who's there?

Butter!

Butter who?

Butter not get into trouble this summer!

What's black and white and red all over?

A sunburned zebra!

Why couldn't the baseball fans drink soda at the double header?

The home team lost the opener!

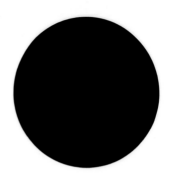

What do you get from an

Alaskan cow?

Ice cream!

☆

Why do you take a baseball player camping?

To pitch the tent!

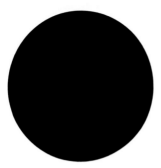

Why did the fish blush?

Because it saw the lake's bottom!

Why is a chicken like a baseball umpire?

They both have fowl mouths!

How hot is it?

So hot that the chickens are laying omelettes!

Can a frog jump higher than a tree?

Of course! A tree can't jump!

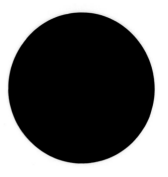

What color is the wind?

Blew!

Knock, Knock!

Who's there?

Marsha!

Marsha who?

Marsha-mallows roasting on a campfire!

Why did the baseball player go to the car salesman?

He wanted a sales pitch!

Knock, Knock!

Who's there?

Annie!

Annie who?

Annie more marshmallows around here?

Knock, Knock?

Who's there?

Dewey!

Dewey who?

Dewey have any more marshmallows?

Have you heard the joke about

the skunk in the woods?

It really stinks!

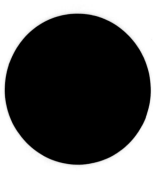

How do you get down from a tree?

You don't! You get down from a duck!

What did the bacon at the picnic say to the

tomato?

Lettuce get together!

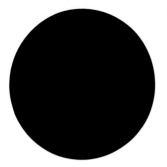

Knock, Knock!

Who's there?

Ken!

Ken who?

Ken you play baseball?

Why do trees have so many friends?

They branch out!

Why are hiking shops so interesting?

They have people from all walks of life!

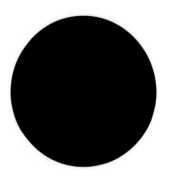

Why are singers good at baseball?

They have perfect pitch!

Where does a whale go to have his teeth straightened?

The orca-dontist!

What do you call the boss of the fish mafia?

The cod-father!

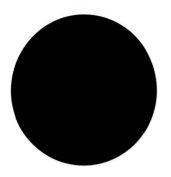

What is a tree's favorite drink?

Root beer!

Why did the robot take a vacation at the beach?

To recharge his solar batteries!

Why did the man love his barbecue?

It was the grill of his dreams!

What did the beaver say to the tree?

It's been nice gnawing you!

How hot is it?

So hot that the squirrels are using

pot holders to pick up nuts!

What race is never run?

A swimming race!

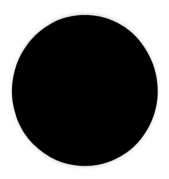

What looks like half a tree?

The other half!

☆

How do you avoid being swallowed by a river?

Stay away from its mouth!

☆

How do you cool down a hot puppy?

Give it a pup-sicle!

☆

Where does a boat go when it is sick?

To the Dock!